How to Spot
The Hidden Psychopaths
In Your Life

A Book Web Mini Exclusive

By Dr. Jeri Fink

How To Spot The Hidden Psychopaths In Your Life
By Dr. Jeri Fink

Published by Book Web Publishing, LTD
Book Web Minis
All rights reserved
Copyright 2019

No part of this publication may be reproduced, stored in or introduced into a retrieval system, or transmitted, in any form, or by any means (electronic, mechanical, photocopying, recording, or otherwise), without the prior written permission of the author and/or publisher.

Cover art by CoverDesignStudio.com

ISBN# 9781799153764

Although the author and publisher have made every effort to ensure that the information in this book was correct at press time, the author and publisher do not assume and hereby disclaim any liability to any party for any loss, damage, or disruption caused by errors or omissions, whether such errors or omissions result from negligence, accident, or any other cause.

This book is not intended as a substitute for the advice of mental health professionals. The reader should consult a mental health professional in matters relating to his/her mental health and social relationships, particularly with respect to any symptoms that may require diagnosis or treatment.

Read cutting-edge Book Web Minis

Book Web Minis are fun, fast, and hot. Mini books (50-80 pages) explore up-to-the-minute facts, photos, content, quizzes, and fiction. Share with friends, family, and colleagues: get them in print or eBook from Amazon.com.

Book Web Minis: www.bookwebminis.com

Bestselling Titles:
Paranormal Is My Normal
Selfies: Picture Perfect
Timepieces I: Yesterday's Stories Today
SOARING
Pocket Cash: Your Happy Money
The Old Lady Who Went To Sleep and Woke Up Young

Look for full-length fiction about psychopaths at
www.hauntedfamilytrees.com

To Ricky and our beloved grandchildren:
John, Nick, Mason, and Emma

Special thanks to the people who supported me in this work:

Nancy Allegretti
Fern Friedman
Mary Ann and Pat Hannon
Craig Hensley
Janet and Rich Kam
Bill Kumar
Jerry and Jill Lash
Herb Michelson
Marge Mendel
Donna Paltrowitz
Shari Paltrowitz
John Violas

And my readers:

Rich Fink
Fern Friedman
Liz Psaltis

How To Spot The Hidden Psychopaths In Your Life

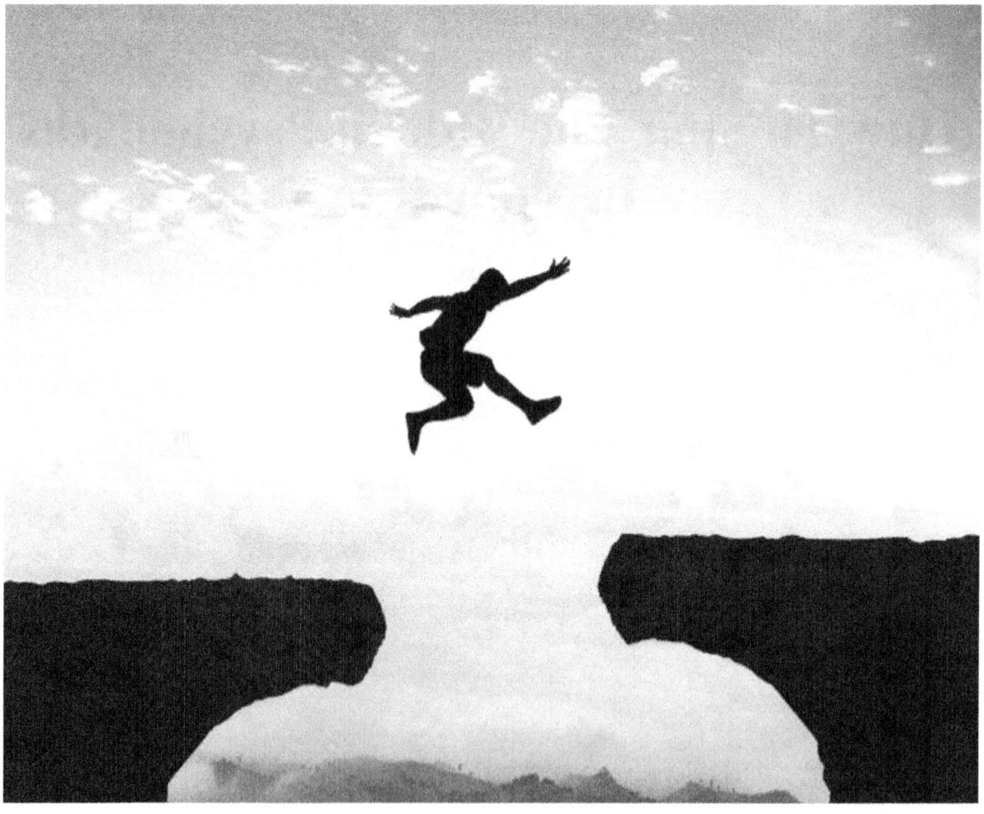

10	How to spot hidden psychopaths
13	Welcome to the Spectrum
17	Hiding in plain sight: Psychopathic traits
21	Where are *you* on the Spectrum?
22	Inside the mind of hidden psychopaths
26	What does conscience and empathy have to do with it?
31	Hidden psychopaths at work
37	What are the best careers for hidden psychopaths?
52	Can hidden psychopaths love?
57	Hidden psychopaths in the bedroom
59	Quotes by or about famous psychopaths
61	Can you spot the hidden psychopaths? A quiz

How to spot hidden psychopaths

Psychopaths. You love to hate them and hate to love them. Movies, TV, books, and the internet are filled with them – creepy, scary murderers who relish violence. They're great on large screens with tubs of buttered popcorn on your lap.

Research has shown that most people enjoy the tension created in mystery and horror. They key in on what's relevant – from the fear of a dark neighborhood or creaking stairs in a too-quiet house. The best part is that it's all fiction; the psychopath probably won't be climbing into your window any time soon.

The truth is a bit more complicated.

Most people don't act like psychopaths in the movies. Others wish they could – at least some of the time. The vast majority of psychopaths don't murder and mutilate. They live in plain sight at work, home, in your building, or neighborhood.

In this book I call them hidden psychopaths because they *seem* to function just like the rest of us. They're great actors and easily imitate anything from speech styles to seductive behavior.

The secret lies beneath the surface.

They simply don't care.

Psychopaths don't worry about what others think or say. They don't feel guilt or responsibility; they do whatever they please, charming, manipulating, lying, and coercing others.

You find them during Happy Hour, in the house next door, and in bed with you. They're friends, family, colleagues, and associates.

In a recent study, Dr. Leistedt and Dr. Linkowski proved this concept. They studied whether fictional psychopaths give us an accurate picture of the real thing. They concluded that while the depiction of psychopaths has become more accurate in recent years, it's still mostly fiction.

In other words, the maniacal laugh, emotional outbursts, and mutilating beautiful young blondes is usually only on the screen.

Psychopaths are cold, unaffected by others, narcissistic, and excellent manipulators. They're in your daily life, although you might not spot them. They don't have to be serial killers to have psychopathic traits – especially in our culture that admires and validates so many psychopathic behaviors. Ironically, psychopathic traits are often the key to success in modern society.

You might even own some of these traits.

Experts refer to this as the Psychopathic Spectrum.

This mini book will guide you through the Psychopathic Spectrum; psychopathic traits that work, leading to success, and traits that harm others. It's a mixed bag. It will give you an understanding of the biology as well as the behavior. It will help you see how and why hidden psychopaths thrive in plain sight.

You'll learn how to spot psychopathic traits in friends, co-workers, neighbors, lovers, and even your own family.

You'll also learn how to live with them.

Hidden psychopaths are often defined as "good or functional" people who score high in traits on the Spectrum. They are not the murderers or bizarre criminals you see in movies or on TV.

Although you or someone you know might have a few psychopathic traits unless they're relatively high on the Spectrum it doesn't dominate their behavior. It's the difference between having a glass of wine at dinner, a problem drinker, and a full-blown alcoholic.

"When I made you VP of Royal Treasury,
I expected you to approve my expense reports."

Welcome to the Spectrum

The CEO takes action. *Profits are down. The price of stock is dropping. The CEO closes a few industrial plants, fires thousands of workers, and moves manufacturing to Mexico. He goes home, hugs his children, and doesn't think (or feel guilty) about it.*

She's a world-renown cardiac surgeon. *As she cuts into the high-risk anesthetized patient on the operating table, she doesn't care about who he is or his family waiting nervously outside. There's a job to be done as quickly and as efficiently as possible. She's in total control.*

He faces twenty thousand people in a political rally. *They want to hear everything he's doing to help them. He lies. He makes up statistics, stories, and taunts his opponents. The crowd loves it. They cheer wildly. Even though he's a multi-millionaire, he persuades the working class crowd that he's one of them. He can convince them of anything.*

The CEO has no empathy for his workers. The surgeon has no emotional attachment to her patient except to succeed at her risky work. The politician will say anything – even lie – to get the power and hero worship he craves.

They're all psychopathic traits – lack of empathy, shallow or no emotional attachments, grandiosity, and no conscience. Yet the CEO keeps his company successful; the surgeon saves her patient's life; and the politician gets elected.

In today's world, having psychopathic traits may not always be a bad thing.

"Psychopath up." says Dr. Kevin Dutton, a world renowned expert on psychopathy at Oxford University "A bit of localized psychopathy is good for all of us."

Huh? Your first reaction might be that Dutton, a highly respected research psychologist and author of many books on the subject, including *The Wisdom of Psychopaths: What Saints, Spies, and Serial Killers Can Teach Us About Success*, might have had one too many servings of bangers and mash.

Think again.

Let's look at it from a different angle. Few things in life are black and white. Most of us live in the muddy waters of gray – a little of this and of little of that.

Dr. Dutton describes *The Psychopathic Spectrum* - a scale that measures the number of psychopathic traits in an individual. As in any scale or range, a person can have a few traits (mild) to so many that it dominates their personality and behavior. Serial killers fall at the extreme range of the Spectrum. The CEO, surgeon, and politician fall at different (lesser) points.

Think of it this way. You love wine. Whenever you go out for dinner you order a glass of Chardonnay. A friend loves wine too, and insists on having a glass at *every* dinner - home or in a restaurant. Another has wine at lunch and dinner *every day*. And yet another starts drinking in the morning and continues all day. Your one glass to drinking all day is a wide range of behaviors – enjoying a glass to alcoholism.

Apply that concept to the Spectrum.

Dutton maintains that psychopathic traits fall on a scale that balances frequency and severity (like the wine). Some of the most distinctive psychopathic traits are ruthlessness, fearlessness, ability to charm and manipulate others, and lack of empathy and conscience. Let's flip that. What if ruthlessness translates into decisiveness; fearlessness into coolness under pressure; manipulation into charisma; and lack of empathy and conscience into the ability not to take things personally?

The CEO who lays off thousands of people and saves his company is clearly ruthless and decisive. The surgeon who rescues her risky patient's life is fearlessness or coolness under pressure. The politician's manipulation and lies is lack of conscience but says what his constituents want to hear (and gets him elected). All three are highly successful.

Dutton's *functional or good psychopathy* has more do with *how* psychopathic traits affect an individual rather than their actual existence. Simply put, a functional or good psychopath can be very useful in today's world – the kind of person you might need someday.

Ask yourself a few questions. Do you want a ruthless (decisive) CEO to run the company where you own stock or someone who can't make up his or her mind? Do you want a focused surgeon, cool under pressure (fearless) without emotions that may hinder her work or someone who is worrying about what the family thinks as she cuts into the patient? Do you want a leader who can use his charm to manipulate legislators into taking action or someone so worried about his or her colleagues that nothing ever gets done?

There's a lot of research on these questions. If psychopathy is not an "all or none" condition, and most psychopaths are *not* violent, maybe we need to rethink Dutton's Spectrum. We don't want Ted Bundys and Jeffrey Dahmers in our midst but what about tough business leaders, focused surgeons, and thick-skinned politicians who get the job done?

Life isn't black and white; we live in shades of gray that might be good, bad, or something in-between. Neither good or bad actions totally define you (unless you're a serious criminal). You make simple and complex choices every day – should you continue a one-sided relationship; is that chocolate chip cookie worth breaking your diet; is it better to side with the boss instead of your peers? Each decision comes with the weight of conscience and empathy – you're sad about the relationship, you feel guilty about the cookie, and you identify with the workers.

The hidden psychopath is free of these extra emotional burdens, able to get things done without worry. It might not be so bad to have them in the right time or place.

"These guys might want to sting us," Dutton says, "but they might also save our lives."

The five most important things you need to know about the Spectrum

1. **Most psychopaths are *not* murderers.** They're all around us, often successful in careers from blue-collar to high level executives and professionals.

2. **Psychopaths on the Spectrum are everywhere.** They come from all races, cultures, and socioeconomic classes. They have all levels of intelligence, from below average to genius. They grow up in single parent homes, two parent homes, and foster homes. Intelligence, opportunity, and getting a good start enables one to achieve a more functional life with fewer psychopathic traits. In contrast, low intelligence, child abuse, sexual abuse, and trauma make it more difficult.

3. **You've already met someone on the Spectrum.** Some researchers say that 1-2% of the population is on the Spectrum. Others feel it's closer to 4-6%. Although the percentages are statistically low, when you consider the entire U.S. population, that's nearly 2 million people on the Spectrum.

4. **They're all around us.** Dr. Robert Hare, author of *Snakes in Suits: When Psychopaths Go to Work,* writes, "Everybody has met these people, been deceived and manipulated by them, and forced to live with or repair the damage they have wrought." Psychopaths on the Spectrum are everywhere. We idolize fearless, powerful people in business, law, politics, and other professions. We work with them, make love with them, live next to them, and go to parties with them.

5. **Does someone *without* a conscience, like a psychopath, stand out?** Having a conscience *defines* us. We assume that everyone has a conscience. People don't recognize psychopaths because the idea of no or limited empathy, emotions, guilt, or regret is beyond a normal imagination – especially with friends, family members, co-workers, and lovers.

Hiding in plain sight: Psychopathic traits

You've seen them, lived with them, loved them, and hated them. Psychopathic traits are a part of daily life from your friends and family, the neighbor next door, your co-workers, and people on television, online, and the big screen. Many of these traits are familiar – *too* close to home?

Check out the following chart. Do you or anyone you care about have any of those traits? How many? How much does it dominate their personality and behavior?

Common Psychopathic Traits

no conscience
no empathy
lack of remorse or guilt
callous
impulsive
shallow emotions
grandiose
glibness/superficial charm
fearless
ruthless
pathological liar
anger

No responsibility
sexual promiscuity
sexual aggression
sexual violence
multiple marriages
manipulative
parasitic life style
lack of long term goals
aggression over trivialities
need for stimulation

In childhood:
early behavior problems
lack of morals
aggression
lying
juvenile delinquency
conduct disorder
breaking/ stealing things
hurting animals
fighting
bullying

What would a hidden psychopath do? A Quiz

Below you'll find a series of psychopathic traits. Each trait is followed by three behaviors. Can you choose what a hidden psychopath would do? The answers are at the end.

1. Fearlessness
a. A CEO ignores his board of directors and makes a critical decision.
b. A CEO tries to convince his board of directors that they should agree with him.
c. A CEO appeals to the stockholders to say he is a good man.

2. No empathy
a. A politician calls a town meeting to explain why it's necessary to close a local school.
b. A politician closes a local school and announces it after the fact.
c. A politician keeps a local school open when it should be closed.

3. Ruthlessness
a. An office worker refuses the higher paying job because his colleague needs the money.
b. An office worker grabs the higher paying job even though he doesn't need the money.
c. An office worker refuses the promotion because there's not enough status.

4. Grandiosity
a. A salesperson refuses a new job because she knows she's not qualified.
b. A salesperson accepts a new job but explains she has a lot to learn.
c. A salesperson accepts a new job even though she knows she's not qualified.

5. No conscience
a. A man cuts down his neighbor's favorite tree without asking.
b. A man discusses cutting down his neighbor's favorite tree.
c. A man asks permission to cut down his neighbor's favorite tree.

6. Need for stimulation
a. The father of young children buys fireworks for July 4 because it's fun.
b. The father of young children refuses to buy fireworks for July 4.
c. The father of young children watches public fireworks on July 4.

7. Impulsivity
a. A college student refuses to go to a party because it might get out of hand.
b. A college student refuses to go to a party because she doesn't like the people.
c. A college student refuses to go to a party because she found a better one.

Answers: 1a, 2b, 3b, 4c, 5a, 6a, 7c

These answers don't need any explanation. We all live, work, play with, and love hidden psychopaths on the Spectrum.

Where are *You* on the Spectrum?

Many experts believe that we're all somewhere on the Spectrum. In other words, everyone has psychopathic traits to varying degrees. Of course, that's not necessarily *bad*. Certain traits can get you ahead in life, help you negotiate the work and stress, and protect you against people who try to attack or bring you down for their own purposes.

There are hundreds of "tests" on the Internet to self-diagnose psychopathy. They're fun, they shed more light on Spectrum traits, and give you a better idea of what psychopathy means.

These tests are **NOT A DIAGNOSIS!** Use them as fun guides or insights into psychopathic thinking. If you're concerned, go to a professional for diagnosis and treatment.

NEVER ASSUME YOU'RE A FULL-BLOWN PSYCHOPATH FROM THE RESULTS OF THESE TESTS.

Remember, what you answer today might be very different from what you would have answered yesterday or tomorrow.

PSYCH CENTRAL
https://psychcentral.com/quizzes/psychopathy-quiz/

BUZZFEED
https://www.buzzfeed.com/tomchivers/where-are-you-on-the-psychopathy-spectrum

LEVENSON SELF-REPORT PSYCHOPATHY SCALE
https://openpsychometrics.org/tests/LSRP.php

DR. DUTTON'S TEST
http://psychopath.channel4.com/quizzes.html

HEALTHY PLACE
https://www.healthyplace.com/psychological-tests/psychopath-test.-am-i-a-psychopath

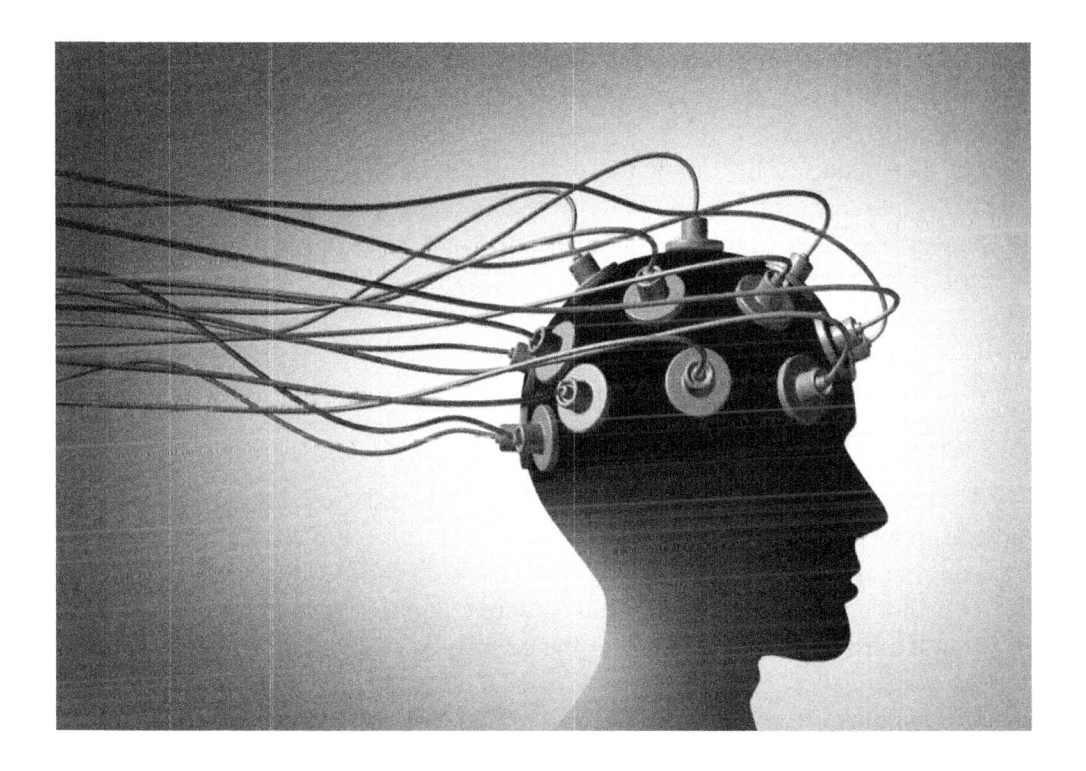

Inside the mind of a hidden psychopath

The brains of hidden psychopaths high on the Spectrum *are* wired differently than the rest of us. Recent studies found a disconnect between the front of the brain (prefrontal cortex) and the amygdala. What does that mean? The prefrontal cortex controls feelings like empathy and guilt; the amygdala reconciles fear and anxiety. According to Dr. William Hirstein, "the brains of psychopaths have been found to have weak connections among the components of the brains emotional systems . . . [probably] responsible for the psychopath's inability to feel emotions deeply."

It's compounded by a tolerance for disgust and the lack of ability to see fear in others. In other words, psychopaths neurologically show shallow or few emotions, particularly shame, guilt, and embarrassment. Their lack of fear and conscience contribute to risk-taking and impulsivity.

Psychopaths usually blame others for their behavior. Non-psychopaths blame themselves. It works for the psychopaths in your life. Add a dose of grandiosity and exaggerated self-worth and the words change.

An excellent example is when Donald Trump bragged, "My IQ is one of the highest and you all know it. Please don't feel stupid or insecure, it's not your fault."

He also claimed he knew more than anyone else about taxes, climate, military, and technology. The list is constantly growing.

Multiple studies found that other psychopath traits are probably related to neurological wiring:

1. Longer time to express emotional facial responses
2. Reduced startle response
3. Immunity to punishment

A study from Vanderbilt University concluded that "these individuals appear to have such a strong draw to rewards . . . that it overrides the sense of risk or concern . . ."

The hidden psychopathic brain is wired to seek rewards at any cost – finding it hard to see or understand the consequences of their behavior.

Do you know anyone like that?

According to Rich Hardy in *Inside the Brains of Psychopaths*, "a lack of empathy, over-acting reward centers, and an inability to evaluate future consequences all line up and lead to one to make a decision that normal people would classify as psychopathic."

Brain wiring – or dysfunctional brain wiring – *may be* the underlying cause of psychopathy. We need more research and more accurate measurements to figure out exactly what happens in psychopathic brains.

Legally, psychopaths are not insane. They don't hear voices or hallucinate. Their thoughts are not disordered or twisted by delusions. They're not psychotic – a feature of mental illness.

Consequently, psychopathy is classified as a personality disorder. They know right from wrong but just don't care. The psychopathic traits on the Spectrum define the disorder:

no conscience
callousness/lack of empathy
lack of remorse or guilt
grandiose sense of self-worth
glibness, and superficial charm
pathological lying
conning/manipulative behavior
shallow emotions.

In addition, psychopaths often fail to accept responsibility, need high stimulation, have a parasitic lifestyle, and demonstrate a lack of realistic long-term goals. These usually show up at a young age as poor behavioral control, early behavioral problems, conduct disorder, adolescent recklessness, criminal tendencies, promiscuous sexual behavior, drug abuse, and later multiple marital relationships.

Whether you have a mild collection of traits or severe symptoms it most likely starts in the brain. The difference between how those traits are expressed – good, functional, bad, criminal – probably is the effects of environment and genetics.

Psychopaths are born with dysfunctional wiring but if they're raised in a strong, healthy environment they have a better chance of being good or functional. In contrast, if they're raised in an abusive, stressful environment, their chances are much worse. Bad parenting, parenting focused on punishment (rather than rewards), negligence, and inconsistency increases poor outcome. Substance abuse by the parents, early parental separation, and lack of parent involvement increases the chances of more traits on the Spectrum.

A psychopath has a better chance of being functional when born and raised in a functional family.

Of course, that's true for all of us.

What does conscience and empathy have to do with it?

Close your eyes and think of your favorite restaurant – the one with a large plate glass window in the front. Now imagine picking up a rock and tossing it into the window, shattering the glass, and sending shards in all directions, perhaps injuring your favorite waiter or waitress, or hurting innocent diners.

How do you feel? Did your heart speed up a bit, or did you feel guilty? Did you frown and think, I could never do that? Was the scene in your head so distasteful that you couldn't wait to get out? That's your conscience talking. It's so automatic that we can even experience it when doing nothing but imagining a behavior.

Now picture a psychopath. He or she wouldn't be at all disturbed about the images. In fact, a psychopath might even think it's a good idea – or a good way to have some fun.

What stops you from really throwing the rock? What compels a psychopath to do it?

Think conscience and empathy – two of the most basic human emotions. Conscience is so fundamental that we often don't realize it's there.

"Since everyone simply assumes that conscience is universal among human beings, hiding the fact that you are conscience-free is nearly effortless." *Martha Stout, Ph.D. The Sociopath Next Door*

What is conscience?
It's an inner feeling or voice – an intuition or judgment – that enables people to tell right from wrong. Conscience is a built-in sense, derived from morals, values, principles, and cultural rules; a cognitive guide that tells you when you're to blame and when you're innocent.

Think of it this way. Conscience is self-awareness of your own morals, ethics, and personal feelings of right and wrong. It may be those sickly pangs in your stomach when you yell at a friend (who doesn't deserve it) or the pounding feeling of shame when you verbally attack a child for something you did wrong.

Essentially your conscience represents who you *are*. Pangs of conscience come from your inner voice, directing you when trying to decide the right thing to do.

Movies and TV humorously portray conscience as an angel on one shoulder and a devil on the other. Who do you listen to when you want to finish the whole bag of cookies, play hooky from work, or refuse to return a text to someone you don't like?

Conscience also plays a broader role in your life. What political candidate or party do you support? Do you follow the tenets of any religion? Which charities do you favor and if any, donate time and money?

Conscience silently creeps into almost every decision and behavior in your life.

Empathy emerges from conscience. Empathy reflects your feelings or identification with the struggles or joys of others. Animal lovers feel empathy for their pets or wildlife, "imagining" (anthropomorphizing) their experiences. Whether for animals or people, empathy is an emotional response *inside* you. It can lead to things like sympathizing with a friend's anger over losing her job, sharing the joy in a colleague's new romance, or helping a child deal with a schoolyard bully. It might make you grieve for wildlife going extinct from climate change; refugees fleeing drug lords; or victims of disease. Empathy impacts conscience and may compel you to vote (or protest) a crooked politician; grieve for impoverished families seeking asylum; or sympathize with a crime victim you "met" on social media.

Conscience and empathy enhance the arts. You might cry watching a sad movie, laugh with a television family, or shiver over fictional stories in books, magazines, and social media. A war photo might make you feel angry, music may sound haunting, and a painting stir emotional reactions. That's the artist "talking" to you and creating empathy within the emotional content of their work.

Conscience and empathy are central to who we are. Without it we couldn't relate to others, understand why someone is smiling, comfort a child's hurts, experience happiness, grief, joy and excitement. We wouldn't be *human*.

Most of us couldn't throw that brick through the window even if we wanted!

What about conscience and empathy in psychopaths?
Many people believe that a psychopath's greatest emotional deficit is lack of conscience and empathy. The hidden psychopath might be able to fake it but you eventually figure out the truth. Here's why. In a study done by Schalwijk, et.al, they found that conscience regulates a wide range of emotions, including "empathy, shame, pride, guilt, and moral judgments."

Apply that to throwing the brick through the restaurant window. You feel guilty just thinking about it. The psychopath, without conscience, might be proud that they can not only throw the brick but get away with it. They don't empathize with the owners or any potential victims and never consider the consequences.

That's hard to miss.

If you have conscience and empathy, you might try to intervene. If you're not there – or fast enough – impulsivity kicks in and you know exactly where the psychopath is headed.

Consider another scenario. The restaurant scene is in a movie; the brick thrower is your hero. Maybe the burger for dinner was overcooked or the service slow. Either way, *watching* the movie you cheer on your hero without a pang of guilt or remorse. You might grin when the sound effects of shattered glass make you jump. It's all virtual – but what does that say about *you*? What does that say about our culture that loves cop shows and war movies, intense professional sports, gun play, and TV reports of violent crimes? Do we control our psychopathic impulses by experiencing them vicariously (virtually) or desensitizing ourselves to horror and injustice (in media)?

Now be honest. Do you want a ruthless CEO to run the company where you own stock or someone who can't make up his or her mind? If there's a bomb scare, do you want it investigated by someone who is terrified or someone who is cool under pressure? Do you want your favorite sports team to push through to victory ignoring the pain of the opposing team?

Doesn't someone *without* a conscience stand out?
Having a conscience defines our species. People don't recognize psychopaths because the idea of no or limited conscience, empathy, emotions, guilt, or regret is beyond a normal imagination – especially when you're dealing with a friend, family member, co-worker, neighbor, or lover.

Yet there are highly functional hidden psychopaths like President Theodore Roosevelt, one of America's most beloved leaders. Researchers determined that TR had the most psychopathic traits of all U.S. Presidents (Donald Trump was not included in the study).

Teddy Roosevelt was known as a commander of the *Rough Riders* – the first U.S. Volunteer Cavalry – famous for his exuberant personality, wide range of interests, stellar achievements, and powerful leadership. Roosevelt won the presidency in a landslide, created the National Park system (and consequently conserved over 230 million acres of federally protected land), helped build the Panama Canal . . . the list goes on, still positively affecting our lives today.

His psychopathic traits were a large part of his success.

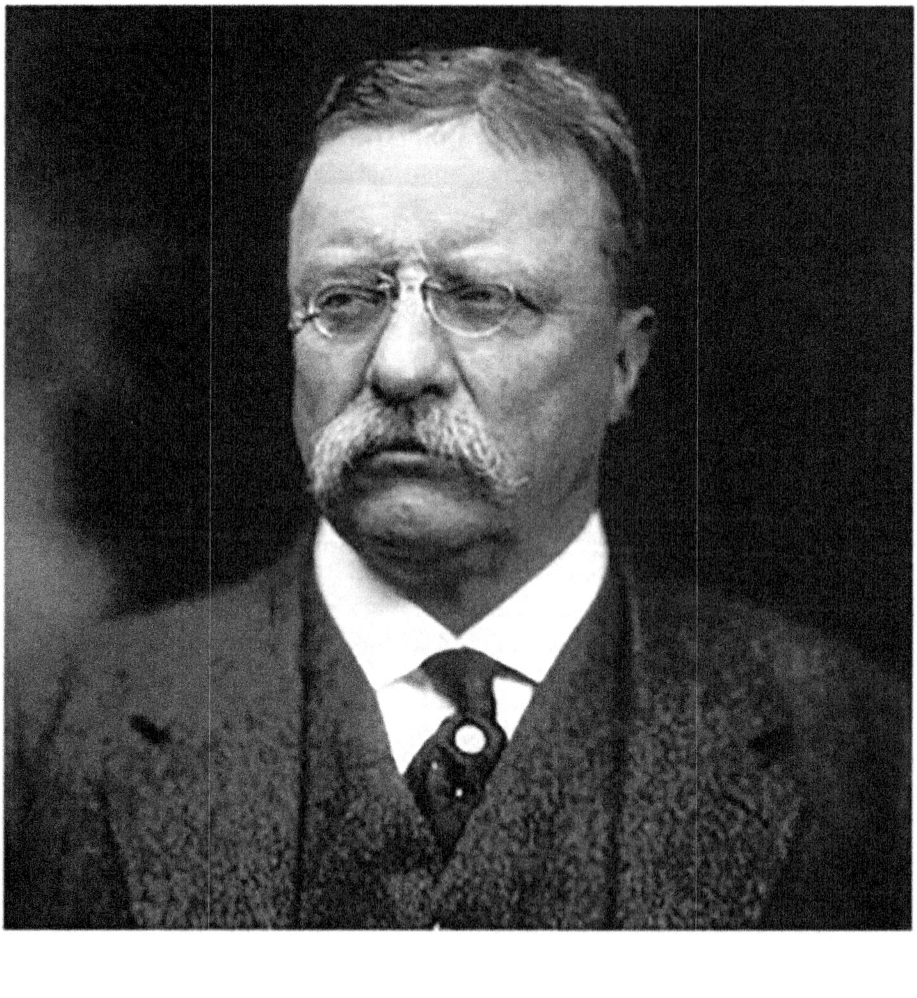

Hidden psychopaths at work

They're superficially charming, self-centered, and ruthless. They have no guilt and don't care about what others think. At the same time, hidden psychopaths can be decisive, risk-taking, and reckless. They *know* how to use their psychopathic traits to get ahead. That's very far from the popular view of psychopaths as creepy guys on TV who torture, murder, and store their victim's head in the refrigerator.

In today's world that might even land you a great job.

What if you have no empathy and easily push people out of your way to get ahead at work, while outside the office you're a loving partner? Maybe you argue endlessly with co-workers while at home you're a gentle, patient parent? What if ruthlessness translates into decisiveness; fearlessness into coolness under pressure; manipulation into charisma; and lack of empathy and conscience into the ability *not* to take things personally?

Perhaps it's not so bad to have "psychopath" in your resume?

Just don't write it in the job description.

Dr. Kevin Dutton, author of *The Good Psychopath's Guide to Bossing Your Life: How to Own Your Day-to-Day the Psychopath Way* writes, "If you have only psychopathic traits you'd be like the serial killers on TV. If you have only a few very useful traits, it might help you become successful. A functional or "good" psychopath can be very important in today's world – the kind of person we might need."

Can you guess which jobs require the most – or least – psychopathic traits?

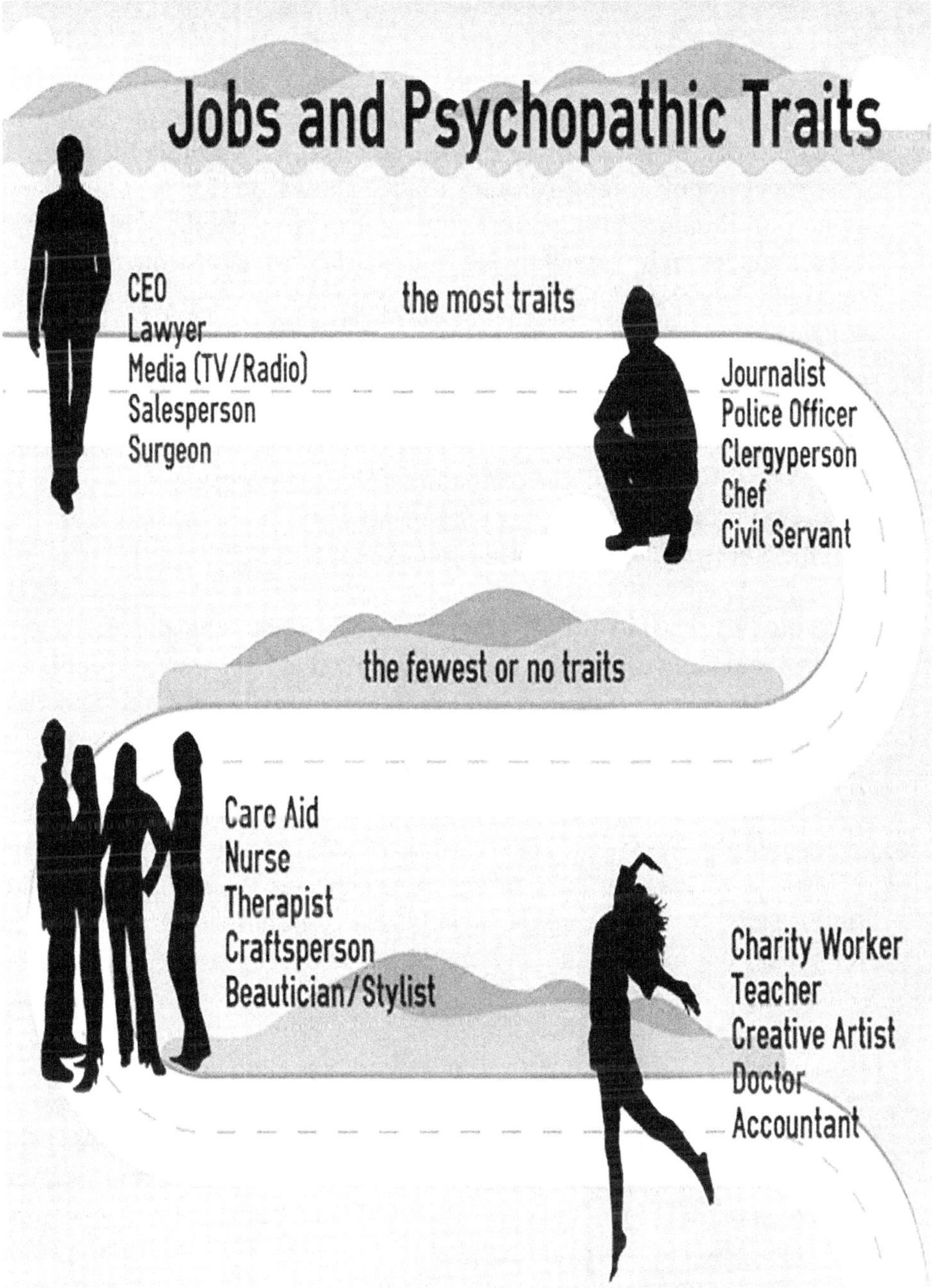

Jobs and Psychopathic Traits

the most traits

- CEO
- Lawyer
- Media (TV/Radio)
- Salesperson
- Surgeon
- Journalist
- Police Officer
- Clergyperson
- Chef
- Civil Servant

the fewest or no traits

- Care Aid
- Nurse
- Therapist
- Craftsperson
- Beautician/Stylist
- Charity Worker
- Teacher
- Creative Artist
- Doctor
- Accountant

The top five jobs for hidden psychopaths

CEO: The best business people are ruthless, narcissistic, and risk-taking. That's why we often describe them as cutthroat or calculating - people who make a killing in the market. It's no accident that one of the most popular, long-running reality shows on TV is *Shark Tank*, where millionaire/billionaire Kings of Business decide which people can make it rich. Can you see the shark's psychopathic traits? It's estimated there are four times as many hidden psychopathic CEOs and business leaders than in the general population.

Lawyer: Many people stereotype lawyers as liars and cheats, obsessed with power, money, getting rich off exorbitant fees, and not interested in the little person – all psychopathic traits. Research has supported the stereotype for a small percentage of lawyers; there are more of them on the Spectrum than any other job except CEOs.

Media (TV/radio/film): Everyone knows about the paparazzi who follow and taunt celebrities or news people that hang out on front lawns to get sound bytes. Clearly, not *everyone* in media is on the Spectrum but if you think of the big personalities in the field it makes a lot of sense that this is the third best job suited for hidden psychopaths.

Salespeople: We've all been victims of salespeople who try to sell us useless products at inflated prices. A salesperson on the Spectrum takes it one step further – he or she is narcissistic, grandiose, and shows little empathy. It's hard to find anyone who hasn't been conned, one way or another, by these guys.

Surgeon: Consider health care workers who have the *fewest* psychopathic traits. Why is a surgeon different? Many surgeons are narcissists who offer two choices: my way or the highway. Add that cutting into human flesh requires a thick skin, steady hand, and not much empathy. If you have any doubts, check out some of television's medical shows where interns and residents fight over the most interesting cases. Is the screen imitating real life? These traits have nothing to do with the quality or skill of a surgeon, only his or her personality. After all, if he or she had too much empathy, felt every cut made into a patient, the result would be a lousy surgeon.

Five more jobs ideal for hidden psychopaths

Can you figure out why?

1. Hi-power journalist (TV anchor, investigative reporters, highly-paid documentarians)
2. Chief of Police
3. Evangelist (television or in person, usually with a lot of money, followers, and audiences that fill giant-sized stadiums)
4. Chef (especially those with national or international fame, television shows, multiple cook books, and experiences with celebrities)
5. Top government workers who control specific areas (think Cabinet Secretaries appointed by Presidents and Governors, and mayors)

Ten jobs that are *terrible* for hidden psychopaths

Can you figure out why?

1. Beautician/Stylist
2. Therapist
3. Teacher
4. Artist
5. Accountant
6. Charity worker
7. Craftsperson
8. Creative artist
9. Non-surgical doctor
10. Stylist

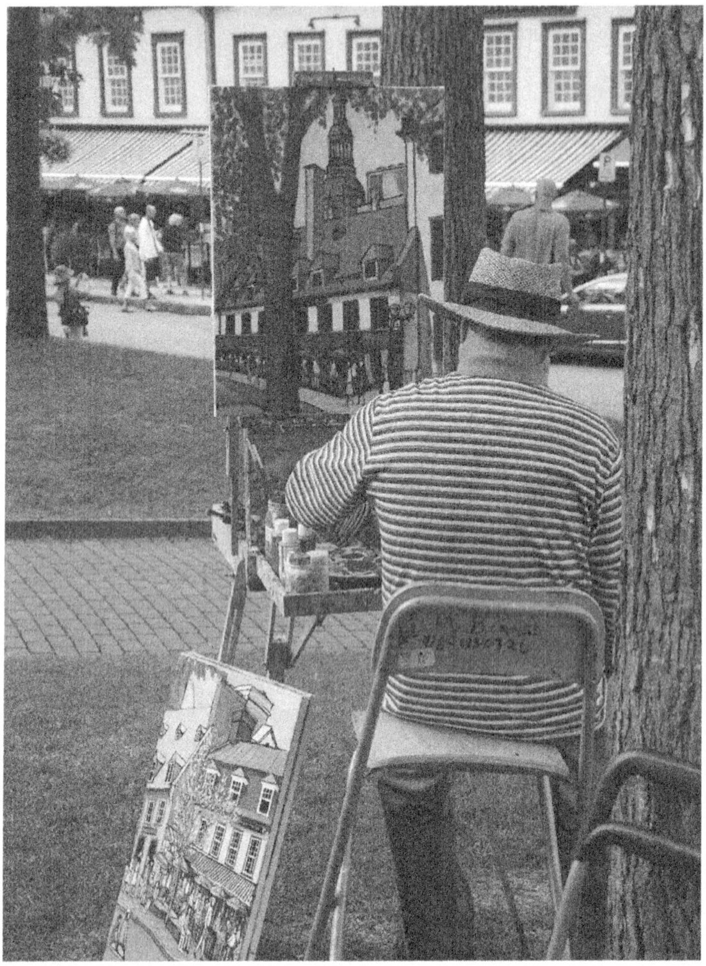

What are the best careers for hidden psychopaths?

U.S. Presidents

CEOs and top business leaders

Elite athletes

Politicians

Trolls, selfies, and psychopaths

U.S. Presidents*

In some jobs, psychopathic traits mean success. Hidden psychopaths, with the right combination of traits, can rise to the top of their fields. With this in mind, Dr. Scott Lilienfeld and Dr. Steven Rubenzer conducted a study on the best (although many think it's the worst) job in the country: Commander-in-Chief.

They distributed personality tests to presidential historians and scholars of every U.S. President, up to George W. Bush. The experts "answered" for their subjects. Lilienfeld and Rubenzer combined personality and performance to estimate psychopathic traits.

The critical factor was "fearless dominance" – defined by boldness, charm, dominance, ability to take control, and coolness in crisis. They were correlated with higher ratings of performance, leadership, persuasiveness, crisis management, and congressional relations. Below are the results. Who would have guessed that the "Rough Rider" and "Teddy Bear" came in first?

Top Ten Presidents with Fearless Dominance

1. Theodore Roosevelt
2. John F. Kennedy
3. Franklin D. Roosevelt
4. Ronald Reagan
5. Rutherford B. Hayes
6. Zachary Taylor
7. Bill Clinton
8. Martin Van Buren
9. Andrew Jackson
10. George W. Bush

*The study did not include Barack Obama and Donald Trump. If it had, President Trump would probably top the list with fearless dominance and other Spectrum traits such as grandiosity, narcissism, chronic lying, and lack of empathy.

Fearless dominance unchecked

FDR turned away thousands of Jewish refugees escaping the Holocaust, suggesting they were Nazi spies (1939).

Donald Trump "helped" suffering Puerto Ricans (after Hurricane Maria) by throwing paper towels at them (2017).

Ronald Reagan was embroiled in the Iran-Contra affair, where weapons were secretly sold to Tehran and the proceeds used to fund Contra rebels in Nicaragua (1985).

John F. Kennedy was in constant scandals about his relationships with women, most notoriously Marilyn Monroe (1962).

Theodore Roosevelt helped organize a revolution that overthrew the government of Panama and replaced it with a nation whose constitution had been written by Americans. The goal was to enable the U.S. to purchase the Panama Canal Project from the French (1903).

CEOs and top business leaders

Let's revisit our business scenario. You own a lot of shares in a company. Would you rather have a CEO that discusses each point in unnecessary detail to make everyone happy? Or a CEO that makes hard, ruthless decisions that ensure success and higher profits?

The second CEO is likely to make you richer. You hope.

You have to be fearless, ruthless, manipulative, and charming to compete in big business. If you fear the competition, bow to the stockholders and critics, and refuse to take risks, you won't make it. You can't have strong conscience or empathy if you have to lay off 10,000 people to become more profitable or slash benefits for poor employees to cut insurance costs. Add necessary grandiosity, narcissism, coolness under pressure, and mental toughness to the mix. You refuse to let anyone stop you from making important decisions because you *know* you're the best.

"*I'm, like, a really smart person.*"- Donald Trump

These hidden psychopathic traits make you loved and hated; give you the fearlessness to do the job that most of us couldn't attempt.

Several studies have shown that the job of CEO requires more psychopathic traits than any other career. No surprise. Either you "have it" or you don't. A CEO with a lot of psychopathic traits can be considered functional – he or she doesn't go around killing people. Returning to our original question - what kind of CEO would you prefer in a company where you own a lot of shares? The answer is simple. You *want* a powerful, successful leader bursting with hidden psychopathic traits.

Unless they go wrong.

We *love* those traits in our business leaders. They make us feel safe, calm, and confident that our money is in the right place. It's risky business. Someone like Bernie Madoff can easily come along and blow our illusions. Madoff could be the poster child for hidden psychopaths gone bad. He had everyone charmed - convinced that he could make big money for them. No one was protected from his $65 billion Ponzi scheme - family, friends, respected colleagues, and charities. He didn't care.

People gave up their money to this "kindly," charming financier. After Madoff's scheme was exposed, his wife was left destitute, one son committed suicide, the second son died from a relapse of cancer that many attributed to stress, and his brother Peter was sentenced to ten years in prison. Leading foundations and charities were brought to their knees, individuals went bankrupt. Madoff was sentenced to 150 years in prison, with a release date of November 14, 2139.

If it wasn't for the economic crash that had nothing to do with him, Madoff would still be in business. Before you malign his victims - great and small - think about the following situations.

What would you do?

1. You're on the Board of Directors of a large, well-established company. Your colleagues are retired executives and great financiers, but old-fashioned. You need a new CEO. Do you choose a person who:
  a. reflects the philosophy of the board and is willing to keep the company in place.
  b. wants to jump into the job with his new ideas rather those of the board.

2. You have money to invest. You choose a professional who:
  a. tells you to be conservative and keep your money in the bank at a low interest rate.
  b. promises you big (hard to believe) returns on your investment.

3. You're watching a weekly television show on finance. Which do you prefer:
  a. The show with a panel of serious men and women in suits and ties who use words you don't understand.
  b. The show with a hyper guy without a tie who promises that if you listen to his advice, you'll make a ton of money.

4. You're asked to invest money for your favorite foundation, raised from a recent fundraiser. Do you:
  a. speculate on what will increase the charity's investment.
  b. listen to other trusted charity investors and follow their suggestions.

If you chose "b" for all or most of your answers, you're like the rest of us. You want to make money in the fastest, easiest way.

#4 is the trick question: if you were smart and took the advice of your peers in what you assumed were safe investments, you might have brought your organization into Bernie Madoff's lethal web.

Where is Bernie Madoff now?

Madoff is serving a 150-year sentence in a medium security federal prison in North Carolina. Steve Fishman, a journalist who hosted a television series about Madoff described him as a "star" in prison. "He stole more money than anyone in history, and to other thieves, this makes him a hero."

Madoff helps other inmates with financial advice and understanding legal issues (Madoff is not a lawyer). But some things never change. He decided to corner the hot chocolate market in prison, buying up every package of *Swiss Miss* in the commissary. Then he sold it for a profit in the prison yard.

According to Fishman, "he monopolized hot chocolate! He made it so that, if you wanted any, you had to go through Bernie."

"My last comment 'appeared' to be inviting feedback. Do not be fooled."

Why do elite athletes make effective psychopaths?

What's a really effective psychopath? There's ruthlessness, fearlessness, decisiveness, ability to charm and manipulate others, and lack of empathy and conscience. What if ruthlessness translates into determination to be number one at all costs? How about if fearlessness becomes taking on tough challenges and decisiveness means never giving up? Add coolness under pressure, lack of empathy or not caring what others think, and you have an ideal *elite* athlete.

Many of us have *some* of those traits; some wish we had more. To be a top athlete – elite in your game - you need to navigate the grueling demands of training, competition, fans, coaches, and ruthless media.

Ever wonder what it's like to walk out on a football field with 50,000 people booing *or* cheering you? Imagine how it feels to be caught doping when the entire world has been celebrating your superhuman achievements – especially when you might *need* drugs to make it happen. What's it like when thousands of media people, sports news commentators, bloggers, and fans analyze your batting slump? If you don't care too much; if you keep your cool; if you *know* you're number one; you can take it all in stride.

Surviving sports celebrity in our world requires an athlete to be a superstar loaded with psychopathic traits. Sometimes it doesn't work – or breaks down too quickly. Consider these three athletes whose psychopathic traits got out of control.

Lance Armstrong Who was a better role model than Lance Armstrong? As a cancer survivor, the cyclist beat all odds to come back and win the *Tour de France* seven times in a row. Who knew that behind his charm, Armstrong was ruthless, callous, and remorseless? After his 10-year doping scheme was revealed, Armstrong claimed "that it was impossible to win the Tour de France in my time without doping." Maybe he was right, but did it include pathological lying and stepping on everyone who stood in his way? He destroyed reputations without guilt or empathy, claiming innocence so he could hang on to the top. Even today, after being disgraced, stripped of his titles, and ordered to pay $10 million to SCA Promotions for lying, Armstrong has no regrets. Oliver Brown wrote in *The Telegraph,* "Whether it is doping past or a recent traffic accident, [this] disgraced American seems unable to accept responsibility." Now Armstrong runs very successful businesses, is involved in several charities, and has a net worth valued at $60 million.

Aaron Hernandez started out as a public hero. As an incredibly talented NFL tight end, he held a $40 million contract with the New England Patriots. It all crashed when Hernandez was charged with murder after a nightclub scuffle. Did Hernandez think he could get away with it - or just didn't care? "They were stalked," the DA said of the victims, "ambushed, and senselessly murdered." Aaron was convicted and sentenced to life in prison without the possibility of parole. He hung himself in prison at age 27.

Tiger Woods showed us incredible talent – along with grandiosity, lack of empathy, and pathological lying. The psychopathic traits became part of Tiger's unbeatable stats when the world's greatest golfer was toppled from his throne. Married to a beautiful woman, the father of two children, Tiger was dubbed a "serial cheater." His sexual liaisons included porn stars, strippers, escorts, party girls, and perhaps his most infamous, a diner waitress. A New York therapist publically stated that "Tiger was embarrassed and ashamed because he got caught, not because he was remorseful." Today Tiger Woods is back on the scene but at a slower, less infamous pace. He runs several businesses and is well known for his charitable Tiger Woods Foundation. His net worth has been estimated at over $760 million.

Can you name other elite athletes who are hidden psychopaths? How many of them are your favorites? What about the owners? How many of them used their psychopathic traits to build fortunes large enough to purchase a sports team?

Are team owners hidden psychopaths?

Most of the sports team owners in the U.S. and around the world made their money before buying their teams. According to Kurt Badenhausen in *Forbes,* team ownership is "the toys of the rich and famous . . . the ticket to billionaire status."

Clearly, these people made their money like most top wealthy business leaders. Are they very successful hidden psychopaths? Let's look at some of their net worth:

Stan Kroenke, $8.8 billion, owner of *LA Rams*
Mark Cuban, $4.11 billion, owner of *Dallas Mavericks*
Stephen Ross, $7.7 billion, owner of *Miami Dolphins*
Philip Anschutz, $11 billion, owner of *Los Angeles Kings*
Daniel Gilbert, $6 billion, owner of the *Cleveland Cavaliers*

Are psychopathic traits required in politics?

You have to be fearless, ruthless, manipulative, and charming to get thousands - millions - of people to wave signs, cheer, work for free, and *follow* you. It's not an easy task unless you're grandiose, narcissistic, don't let anyone stand in your way, and *know* you're the best. They're all typical hidden psychopathic traits that make politicians loved and hated; expected to smile even when under attack; and remain cool in the worst political crises.

In politics, psychopathic traits usually mean success. Hidden psychopaths, with the right combination of traits, seize power if it suits their needs. Think Vladamir Putin, Kim Jong-un and Mohammed bin Salman bin Abdulaziz Al Saud (Crown Prince of Saudi Arabia). Murder, imprisonment, and destroying enemies are all part of their political (psychopathic) leadership.

Let's go American and look at our political leaders – from national to state to local. Are they decisive, cool under pressure, aim for power, and full of fearless dominance?

How does your state governor, mayor, congressperson, or senator operate? They all look good on the screen and in front of local groups. They're smooth-talking and cool in the midst of disasters. We look to them for guidance in the most dramatic collisions in life. We also look to them to show empathy – a performance that many can easily fake.

What's behind the mask – where you can't see who they really are? Why are so many corrupt, living life above the law? Why do so many abuse others behind closed doors?

Not too long ago, a beloved county legislator in my community pleaded guilty to felony mail fraud of over $2 million dollars. Everyone was shocked. The man was so charming –always part of community life. His kids went to the same schools that my kids attended; he showed up at many of my book signings, smiling and offering encouragement. His name was always in the local newspapers, supporting grass roots interests.

What happened? County Legislator David Denenberg was running for New York State Senator – a higher office than the one he held. He was a definite win – who wouldn't support the man? Until he was accused of fictitious client billing, falsified expense submissions, and forging the signatures of federal judges on phony court documents. When the scandal broke, David Denenberg vigorously defended himself against the charges.

A few months later he dropped out of the race for State Senator, resigned his seat in the Nassau County Legislature, and pleaded guilty. Although he withdrew, his name still remained on the ballot.

28,104 people voted for him.

There are many other corrupt politicians in our democracy. Often they're revealed in schemes and behaviors spread across the media; others have been charged of everything from sexism, racism, and anti-Semitism, and still win elections.

Donald Trump was accused by 19 women, confessed to sexual predation on an audio tape heard by the world and still won the presidency; 1 in 4 government officials have been accused of sexual misconduct and remain in office. U.S. Congress set up a slush fund to pay off sexual abuse claims (with taxpayer's money). What is more infamous than the cover-up by Attorney Michael Cohen, publisher David Pecker, and Donald Trump in "catch and kill" schemes to silence women who had affairs with the notorious businessman and President? Or the lies told (and unsuccessful cover-up) by President Bill Clinton's sexual relationship with White House intern, Monica Lewinsky? How about Richard Nixon?

The list is long and treacherous. Political corruption is so rampant that I often wonder if we should re-define it. Ironically, an "innocent" public loves to hear about corrupt politicians and their fall from glory.

There's an old saying – lawmakers make the laws but it doesn't mean they have to follow them.

Trolls, Selfies, and Psychopaths.
What do they have in common?

Who are they? *What* are they?
Strange bedfellows . . . until you really think about it.

Internet trolls are haters. They love to create messes, making you look or feel bad about yourself. The personality traits of trolls include aggression, deception, disruption, and power (through online taunts).
Sound familiar?
Researchers have found that internet trolls show a dreaded personality type known as *The Dark Tetrad*.
You wouldn't want to meet one in a lonely internet alley.

Obsessed Selfies are people who *live* to take selfies. We all know who they are. Some call it the Selfie Syndrome; others say it's a selfie addiction. Mostly male, obsessed selfies are narcissistic, self-involved, and don't care about anyone else's selfie. Some say they show the dreaded personality type known as *The Dark Tetrad*.

Sound familiar?
You wouldn't want to be in a selfie contest with one of them.

Hidden psychopaths are narcissistic, sadistic, lack empathy, ruthless, fearless, and have no conscience. We love them in the movies and hate them if they sit at the next desk. They come from all walks of life - blue and white collar workers to CEOs and professionals. In fields like politics and elite sports, psychopathic traits make them more successful at their work.

Some say they epitomize the dreaded personality type known as *The Dark Tetrad*.

What's the Dark Tetrad?
One of the best ways to understand *The Dark Tetrad* is through a recent, creepy research study. Subjects were given a "bug-crunching" machine that looked like a coffee grinder. They had to drop live pill bugs into the machine, force down the cover, and "grind them up." The bugs came from cups labeled *Muffin, Ike,* and *Tootsie*. The subjects didn't know there was a barrier between the bugs and grinding mechanism. They believed that when the cover was pushed and they heard a gruesome, crunching sound the bugs were killed.

People with high levels of sadism (psychopathy) loved it. The more bugs they crunched, the greater the pleasure – they were happy to inflict suffering.

Does *that* sound like internet trolls and obsessed selfies?

The four personality traits of *The Dark Tetrad*
This dismal personality type is associated with four prevailing psychopathic traits (and bug-crushers):
1. Narcissism, grandiosity, lack of empathy.
2. Machiavellianism, exploitation of others, lack of morality, love of deception.
3. Impulsivity, selfishness, lack of empathy and conscience.
4. Pleasure from causing or observing others to suffer.

Put it all together.
The Dark Tetrad personality type is a well-accepted concept. Some of our most beloved villains emerge from this abyss – The Joker (*Batman*), Professor Severus Snape (*Harry Potter*), Joffrey Baratheon (*Game of Thrones*), and Tony Soprano (*Sopranos*).

Some of our most hated politicians live there as well, like Vladimir Putin, Rod Blagojevich (former Governor of Illinois), and Basjar al-Assad (Syria).

Of course, there are the *others* that most of us hate or fear - even the co-worker that you avoid at all costs.

There's no shortage. We love to hate them, but we don't love to live with them. Unfortunately, we can't imagine life *without* them.

They thrive online. Be warned! Stay away from Internet Trolls, Obsessed Selfies, Psychopaths, and *all* denizens of *The Dark Tetrad*. If you meet someone who fits the bill, click on delete. Fast. You don't want to deal with the online version of hidden psychopaths.

The internet and social media is a perfect place for psychopaths to hang out. There are unlimited victims. It's no accident that Russia set up an army of trolls and chose social media to rig American elections. What about other trolls working for political or religious causes? Most of the time we don't know who they are.

There's an old saying – "on the internet, no one knows you're a dog." It's just as true today as it was years ago.

Be as wary of trolls, obsessed selfie-takers, the dark tetrad, and not-so-well-hidden online psychopaths. They're everywhere, using cat phishing, cyber-attacks, double switches, click baiting, identity thefts, and constantly evolving ways to attack and hurt innocent users.

No one is immune.

Can hidden psychopaths love?

It depends on your definition of love.

Experts, researchers, and victims have hotly debated the question. How can someone with shallow emotions, lack of conscience and empathy, and chronic lying find intimacy?

According to Dr. Seth Myers, *Dr. Seth's Love Prescription,* they can't. "The psychopath simply isn't capable of trusting and depending on another individual . . . as if [they're] part ice."

Many agree. They note that psychopaths tend toward abusive behaviors and patterns in love relationships. The old metaphor, *the eyes are the window to the soul* seems to hold true. Subjective reports describe that looking into a psychopath's eyes is like falling into a dead, bottomless pit, with no expression or life. Some believe that the flat, blank look in the eyes can tell you exactly who they are *inside.*

One study done at Cardiff and Swansea Universities found that psychopaths are bold, confident, and cold-blooded. Their conclusion came from diagnosed psychopaths' response to negative images. Gruesome images that would make most of us turn away or close our eyes, have little or no effect on psychopaths.

It's easy to be bold if you have no fear; cold-bolded in you have no empathy.

Forming relationships requires skills that most psychopaths don't have or can't imitate for too long. They have few, if any, lasting attachments. "Love" can be "pretend" – a performance lifted from other sources rather than the heart.

Their need for constant validation, grandiosity, power, and control becomes a bigger problem as a relationship mellows and intimacy is expected (from the non-psychopath).

The result can be behavior (like lying and infidelity) destined to destroy a relationship. *Gaslighting* creeps in when psychopaths manipulate their partners and slowly break them down until reality and self-esteem is questioned. This pattern is repeated, further shattering the non-psychopath's sense of self. Any objection is usually met with contempt, coldness, or indifference.

Since most of us will assume blame before we recognize it in our psychopathic partners, this creates an unbalanced relationship totally dominated by the psychopath.

That's exactly what the hidden psychopath wants: power, control, and grandiosity. When the inevitable boredom sets in, the psychopath simply finds someone else. Fidelity is not in the playbook; the only important thing is to fulfill their needs without empathy or awareness of their partner's suffering.

Relationships with psychopaths usually end with indifference – while the non-psychopathic partner might be emotionally shattered.

There are many stories, movies, and books about love relationships with psychopaths. "Intimacy" often follows patterns repeated compulsively by the psychopath - strategized behaviors through the life of love relationships.

Hidden psychopathic traits that attract lovers

*Psychopaths are usually charming, well-spoken, attractive and have interesting stories (although many might be lies).

*They appear calm without any stress or anxiety.

*They easily take control of a situation. They're impressive.

*Impulsivity and risk-taking is particularly appealing to people who tend toward safety and seek more excitement in their lives.

*They do different things that might be mildly dangerous and engage both mind and body.

*They're never boring.

*They know (and use) the trappings of romance – sunsets, sweet gifts, movie-style romance techniques – rose petals and candles.

*They tell stories that please and entertain others, inspire respect, and trust (even if the stories are lies).

*They don't feel bad or weigh you down with heavy emotions (unless they're mirroring you).

*They can read, fake, and copy your feelings.

*They never admit blame and behave as if they're very strong and sure of themselves.

*They never do anything wrong (or so they believe).

How hidden psychopaths "pattern" their relationships

There's a general pattern in psychopathic relationships. Keep in mind that every psychopath is different, as with every human being. The pattern may shift in one relationship or set of partners to another.

This is a baseline to understanding what happens when you or someone you care about, gets caught up in a love relationship with a psychopath.

This pattern was described by David Gillespie, *Taming Toxic People: The Science of Identifying and Dealing with Psychopaths At Work and At Home,* and many other researchers studying psychopathic love patterns. The titles are mine.

*Rose petals and candles. It usually begins with a storybook romance filled with Hollywood-inspired words, gifts, and adulation. The first connection is often at a bar or party where people are drinking, their guard is down, and they're more vulnerable to a psychopath's advances. Psychopaths are incredibly skilled at mirroring others so it often feels like you've met a soulmate who knows everything you need or want.

It's as if they're too good to be true and you're incredibly lucky.

*Mirror, mirror on the wall. Psychopaths quickly figure you out. They address your insecurities until it feels like you're the most important person in the world. As skilled actors, they emulate the person that you want them to be. The goal is to gain trust by sharing stories and experiences that are usually lies or exaggerations. They hook you through manipulation and feigned empathy for your problems. This is enhanced by their own "sad" stories – everything from cancer, to lost family, to stolen opportunities in the job market or at work. They use *your* empathy to draw you into their lair.

At this point, many non-psychopaths find themselves deeply in love.

*Look ma, no hands! Once you're snared, the hidden psychopath will bring in others – potential partners, admirers, and one-night stands - to show how lucky you are. It's a reminder that there are many other options besides you. Ironically, others will see the psychopath as charming and capable, often blaming you for any problems. They too, fall for the charisma and manipulation, buying the persuasive behavior even if it includes your failures or limitations. A one-way bond emerges.

Better not slip.

*Caught in the web. Signs start to emerge but you ignore them. You're too much in love. You might catch silly, unnecessary lies; attempts to cut you off from friends and family; encouragements to become dependent while at the same time the psychopath is increasingly parasitic – using your money, your home, and your assets. You pay for almost everything; perhaps constantly loaning money that is never returned. Arguments begin but there's always an excuse, a rationalization, denial, or lie.

It's not their fault . . . it's yours.

*Trapped. You're hooked and your psychopathic partner is bored. You're faced with silence, infidelity, and rejection. You try to rekindle the rose petals and candles but that seems long gone. Sometimes there are multiple outside lovers with no attempt to hide them. If the psychopath senses that you're pulling away there might be a temporary return to trust and adulation to entice you back and repeat the pattern.

It doesn't last long.

*You're out. It becomes clear that you or your relationship isn't working. Your partner is bored and indifferent to your feelings. You might try to hold on longer, convinced it's just a bad phase. As hard as you try, the psychopath doesn't get it (a clear sign of no conscience or empathy). You might become depressed or anxious, unable to figure out what happened. As hard as you try, the blame falls on you.

The end will come as if you never existed, leaving you alone, emotionally shattered, and confused. If it's convenient, the psychopath might keep you around while finding new partners and victims.

It's an awful way to be in love.

Hidden psychopaths in the bedroom

Lack of conscience, lack of empathy, and the hunger for power persists even in the most intimate moments.

*Dr. Seth Meyers writes "Psychopaths [in sex] are chiefly oriented around getting their most important needs met, regardless of the expense to others."

*Psychopaths can be excellent lovers in a "performance" motivated by power and control.

*Sexual promiscuity and infidelity is a given.

*Researchers found that women with poor or few attachments to others seek superficial sexual relationships with psychopaths.

*Psychopaths feel no guilt or consequences if their partner is hurt emotionally or physically.

*Psychopaths learn from movies and TV, play-acting sexual maneuvers without guilt.

*Studies have shown that people who fear intimacy are attracted to the emotionless "safety" of sex with psychopaths.

*Sexual commitment and loyalty isn't important – psychopaths "cheat" easily, whether it's casual or a structured relationship (as in marriage).

*Many view psychopaths as sexual predators.

"Alright, it's agreed. You won't mess with us and Henry won't unleash his toxic self on the world."

Quotes by or about famous hidden psychopaths

"My father was a psychopath . . . he was charming, fearless, ruthless (but never violent) . . . It's a good thing genes aren't everything, right?" - Dr. Kevin Dutton, *The Wisdom of Psychopaths: What Saints, Spies, and Serial Killers Can Teach Us About Success.*

"I don't believe I'm a bad person." - *Bernie Madoff, sentenced to 150 years in prison for a $65 million Ponzi Scheme.*

"In the right context, certain psychopathic characteristics can be very constructive . . . How do you think these great defence lawyers can annihilate an alleged rape victim . . . break [her] down to the extent that she's affected for the rest of her life . . . [and] goes home, cuddles his kids, and goes out for dinner with his wife." - Andy McNab, co-author with Dr. Dutton, *The Good Psychopath's Guide to Success.*

"Not all psychopaths are in prison - some are in the boardroom." - Dr. Robert D. Hare, *Without Conscience: The Disturbing World of the Psychopaths Among Us.*

"Roger Stone explained . . . that Trump's psychic makeup made it impossible for him to take a close look at himself. Nor could he tolerate knowing that somebody else would then know a lot about him and therefore have something over him." - Michael Wolff, *Fire and Fury*

"I return to the fire. It hugs me; orange fingers curl around my hands and arms and legs and chest. Wild flames fill me and power me. There's no stopping me." - Dr. Jeri Fink and Donna Paltrowitz, *Broken By Evil.*

"Psychopaths are skilled at social manipulation, and the job interview is a perfect place to apply their talents." - Paul Babiak, Ph.D and Robert D. Hare, Ph.D, *Snakes in Suits: When Psychopaths Go To Work.*

"I could stand in the middle of Fifth Avenue and shoot somebody, and I wouldn't lose any voters." - *President Donald Trump.*

"Psychopaths get a bad rap — and, in fairness, it's often for good reason. The ones who tend to catch the public eye are known for murdering or, at the very least, manipulating the unwary without remorse. But what about the psychopaths who quietly live among us without raising suspicion?" - James Fallon, *The Psychopath Inside: A Neuroscientist's Personal Journey into the Dark Side of the Brain.*

"Despite the popular perception, most psychopaths aren't coldblooded or psychotic killers. Research suggests many of them live successfully among the rest of us, using their personality traits to get what they want in life." - Scott Lilienfeld and Ashley Watts *for The Conversation, The Daily Mail.com.*

"What makes psychopaths different from all others is the remarkable ease with which they lie, the pervasiveness of their deception, and the callousness with which they carry it out." - Dr. Robert D. Hare, *Without Conscience: The Disturbing World of the Psychopaths Among Us.*

"I think my book offers really good evidence that the way that capitalism is structured really is a physical manifestation of the brain anomaly known as psychopathy." - Jeff Bercovici, *Forbes, Why (Some) Psychopaths Make Great CEOs.*

"I have a gut, and my gut tells me more sometimes than anybody else's brain can ever tell me." - *President Donald Trump.*

"In short, ISIS is composed of religiously motivated psychopaths." - Jay Sekulow, Jordan Sekulow, Robert W. Ash, David French, *Rise of ISIS: A Threat We Can't Ignore.*

"We serial killers are your sons, we are your husbands, we are everywhere." - *Ted Bundy, serial killer.*

Can you spot the hidden psychopaths? A Quiz.

Not all psychopaths are murderers and not all murderers are psychopaths. There are a lot of psychopaths out there who aren't physically violent. There are also a lot of people who have some (but not all) psychopathic traits on the Spectrum. Can you spot the hidden psychopath?

Read the questions below and choose the answer that you believe best describes the hidden psychopath. The correct answers are at the end of the quiz.

1. What does gender have to do with it?
a. Most psychopaths are male.
b. Most psychopaths are female.
c. Psychopaths are equally divided between men and women.

2. What does a psychopath look like?
a. Scary and unfriendly
b. Tongue-tied and embarrassed
c. Normal

3. Which profession is more likely to appeal to a psychopath?
a. Social worker
b. Attorney

4. How do psychopaths see the world?
a. They know right from wrong.
b. They don't know right from wrong.
c. They know right from wrong but don't care.

5. What percentage of the population are psychopaths?
a. 1-2%
b. 10-12%
c. 24-28%

6. What percentage of the population shows psychopathic behaviors?
a. 4-5%
b. 12-14%
c. 26-30%

7. Psychopaths are:
a. Curable
b. Incurable
c. Behavior can be modified but not eliminated

8. Which profession is more likely to appeal to a psychopath?
a. CEO
b. Nurse

9. Which profession is less likely to appeal to a psychopath?
a. Charity worker
b. Nurse
c. All of the above

10. If you think a co-worker or friend is a psychopath you can:
a. Spot him or her a mile away
b. You're more likely to blame yourself for any problems

11. Which is easier?
a. Life with a conscience
b. Life without a conscience

12. The psychopathic Spectrum is a:
a. Rainbow
b. Color chart
c. Scale of psychopathic traits

13. A functional or good psychopath is a:
a. Loser
b. Can be very successful
c. A serial killer

14. Most psychopaths are violent.
a. True
b. False

15. Some psychopathic traits are:
a. Lack of empathy
b. No conscience
c. Grandiosity
d. All of the above

16. Psychopaths are:
a. Impulsive
b. Thoughtful

17. Recent studies have shown that:
a. Psychopathy comes only from the environment
b. Psychopathy is learned
c. Psychopathy is the result of dysfunctional wiring in the brain and the environment

18. If someone has psychopathic traits:
a. No one will want to hire you
b. It might get you a great job

19. Internet trolls are often:
a. Innocent
b. Psychopaths
c. Only Russian

20. Who best utilizes hidden psychopathic traits?
a. Elite athletes
b. Politicians
c. Business leaders
d. All of the above

21. Psychopaths are skilled at:
a. Social manipulation
b. Charming people
c. Pretending to have a conscience
d. All of the above

22. Gruesome images:
a. Don't bother psychopaths
b. Terrify psychopaths
c. Make psychopaths laugh

23. A psychopath's eyes can be:
a. Blank
b. Lifeless
c. Expressionless
d. All of the above

24. Psychopaths in relationships are:
a. Trustworthy
b. Great
c. Manipulative

25. Which psychopathic traits appeal to lovers?
a. Calmness
b. Never boring
c. Impulsive, risk-taking behaviors
d. All of the above

26. Are there hidden psychopaths in your life?
a. Not a chance
b. Probably

Answers:
1a, 2c, 3b, 4c, 5a, 6a, 7c, 8a, 9c, 10b, 11b, 12c, 13b, 14b, 15d, 16a, 17c, 18b, 19b, 20d, 21d, 22a, 23d, 24c, 25d, 26b

15-26 correct answers – you can spot a hidden psychopath.
9-14 correct answers – does your boss, lover, or significant other have a killer instinct you haven't noticed?
8 or below correct answers – read this book again!

Read more about hidden psychopaths!

Book Web's Full-length Fiction series: **BROKEN!**

Amazon #1 Bestsellers

Page turners filled with hidden psychopaths, haunted family trees, strange lovers, and chilling photo insights burst into life. *Broken Books* blend fact, fiction, and photos into riveting stories you'll never forge!
Go to amazon.com to purchase them in eBook, print (black & white), and collector's edition (full color print).

Contemporary:

Broken By Truth (Book 1)
Broken By Birth (Book 2)
Broken By Evil (Book 3)

Historical:

*Broken By Madness (*Book 4, Dutch New Amsterdam, 1654)
Broken By Men (Book 5, Spain and Portugal, 1490s)
Broken By Kings (Book 6, Sao Tome, Africa, 1494)
Broken: The Prequel (Book 7, Spanish Inquisition, 15th century)

for more information click here
www.hauntedfamilytrees.com

click here to Purchase titles on amazon.com
www. https://www.amazon.com/jerifink/ broken books

Dr. Jeri Fink is an author, photographer, and family therapist/clinical social worker. She has worked in mental health and written over 32 nonfiction and fiction books for adults and children. Her articles and blogs appear on and off line, including hundreds of topics ranging from psychology, technology, history, fiction, humor, and family. She wrote the *Broken Series* – seven thrillers set in the 15th century to the present. In *Book Web Minis Series* she explores cutting-edge fiction and nonfiction that affirms the power of positive meaning.

Why Book Web Minis? These books are devoted to sharing nonfiction, fiction, and cutting-edge research in collaboration with leading experts and professionals. Each book is fun, fast, and a window into specific ideas, studies, and stories. The minis are always positive, stressing the best ideas, behaviors, and stories with a "dose of reality."

For more information on individual titles or to purchase Book Web Minis go to:

http://www.bookwebminis.com

To purchase Book Web Minis directly on Amazon go to:
www.amazon.com/gp/bookseries/B07CYLKWJL

To contact Dr. Jeri Fink send an email to:
drjeri@drjerifink.com

To join "Photo Insights" - original feel-good photos delivered weekly, for free, into your email box go to:
http://hauntedfamilytrees.com/landing-page

Although the author and publisher have made every effort to ensure that the information in this book was correct at press time, the author and publisher do not assume and hereby disclaim any liability to any party for any loss, damage, or disruption caused by errors or omissions, whether such errors or omissions result from negligence, accident, or any other cause.

This book is not intended as a substitute for advice of mental health professional. The reader should consult a mental health professional in matters relating to his/her mental health and social relationships, particularly with respect to any symptoms that may require diagnosis or treatment.

Printed in Great Britain
by Amazon